Date Due

921
M

BarryManilow

by Ann Morse
designed by Mark Landkamer

CREATIVE EDUCATION
CHILDRENS PRESS

Published by Creative Education, Inc., 123 South Broad Street, Mankato, Minnesota 56001 Copyright © 1978 by Creative Education, Inc. International copyrights reserved in all countries. No part of this book may be reproduced in any form without written permission from the publisher. Printed in the United States.

Library of Congress Cataloging in Publication Data

Morse, Ann.
    Barry Manilow.

    SUMMARY: A brief biography emphasizing the career of the popular musician and singer.
    1. Manilow, Barry — Juvenile literature. 2. Rock musicians — United States — Biography — Juvenile literature. [1. Manilow, Barry. 2. Musicians] I. Title.
ML3930.M3M7   784'.092'4 [B] [92]   77-24653
ISBN 0-87191-617-7

Photographs:

The young starlet seemed to think that she was pretty hot. And Barry Manilow knew that he was hot. "Actually we were both nobodies," Barry said later. But at that first practice session at the Continental Baths in 1971, it was clear how Barry felt about Bette Midler. Unimpressed. Bette, however, was asked to entertain the patrons of the steam baths and Barry, the best known piano player and arranger in New York, had recently become the regular accompanist. The proprietor thought that the two would make up a good act. But at the practice sessions, Barry was convinced that this new female star would flop the night of the show.

Saturday night came and Barry nearly fell off his piano stool. "I was crying the ballads, laughing at her jokes, playing my tail off at the piano! I was feeling this energy four feet from me — a comet, a meteor." Without difficulty, Barry swallowed his ego and bounded backstage. "Whaa, wow, how did you do that?" he asked Bette.

In minutes, the admiration became mutual. Barry appreciated the power that came from this zany lady. And Bette Midler could see that Barry's arranging ability was exactly what she needed. Though the egos clashed, Barry began to see that maybe they could be good for each other.

That realization wasn't an easy one for Barry, though. It took Barry some time to decide to plunge into such a partnership. He was pretty well known by then as an arranger. He'd worked with other stars on their entrances into the pop world and their ascents up the charts. Barry wasn't sure that he wanted to be the man-behind-the-scenes with another one. Besides, he was beginning to get into his own songwriting.

Yet there was something about Bette that captivated Barry. He felt that Bette was expressing something different, something appealing to the public. And Barry knew that he could clean up Bette's act, give her pacing and arrange her songs to suit her particular style. Finally, he agreed.

Barry set to work doing what he did best — arranging. In a matter of weeks, with Barry's help, Bette's sound emerged into a rich variety of mellow songs from the 1920's, swinging numbers from the 1930's and 1940's, camp-type songs from the 1950's and a smattering of rock pieces from the 1960's. Her act became fresh and new both because of her 1970's interpretation and because of Barry Manilow's modern arrangements. Barry knew how to style Bette's songs so perfectly that they became more than just a repetition of old songs — they became a whole new musical form.

Some musical critics have even credited "The Divine Miss M," as Bette soon came to be called, with opening up the window of all American pop. When most of the world still felt that only rock defined current music, Bette was searching in the closets of music history. She came out making singing statements that nothing was wrong with Broadway hits, old crooning melodies and rock'n roll. Soon people standing on bus stops or behind counters were humming Bette's versions of "Lullaby of Broadway," "Boogie Woogie Bugle Boy," or "Do You Wanna Dance?"

Not only was Barry Manilow involved with this new image Bette Midler was creating; he was much of its inspiration. Yet Barry was doing more than arranging Bette's songs, he was dabbling in songwriting for his own purposes. So when Bette received an invitation to play

8

at the Upstairs at the Downstairs club, Barry wasn't too sure he wanted to be only the accompanist. "The only way I'll do it is if I can sing some of the songs I wrote," Barry told Bette. So he, another singer and a drummer put together a 20-minute opening act of Barry's own numbers. Still, Barry continued to like to arrange for Bette. He would do anything, it seemed, to help her reach her potential.

Johnny Carson was also a help in those beginning days of Bette Midler's career. He considered her a woman of amazing talent, and he had her perform several times on "The Tonight Show." Still, in the beginning, Bette's popularity came mostly from her first two albums.

Ahmet Ertegun, the powerful president of Atlantic Records, heard Bette just once before contracting with her to do a record. Once the agreement was signed, a strange thing happened. The producer didn't know what to do with her.

Atlantic's finest producer, Joel Dorn, was faced with putting on record the sound of a woman who didn't fit into one category. She did pop, boogie woogie, rock, folk, golden oldies, blues— nearly every kind of music.

As her arranger, Barry realized the problem Atlantic was having. At first, he was asked to lay down all the arrangements for Bette's record. He did that; Atlantic thanked him and said good-bye. It was Barry's first opportunity, and he had been ecstatic at the prospect of recording. So he didn't expect it all to fizzle so quickly.

Barry left the recording studio feeling bitter and angry at Bette. "How could you let me leave?" Barry asked Bette. But later he knew the reason— she was scared. It was her first time to record, too.

Meanwhile, Atlantic was keying up to launch Bette Midler's first album in a most extravagant style. Since the album contained many old songs, Joel Dorn lined up top-ranked musicians in the worlds of rock, rhythm-and-blues, old-time swing and big bands to do back-up music. Movie stars, like Bette Davis and Joan Crawford, were asked to read narratives to link the old songs together.

But it wasn't working. Eight months after they started, Atlantic knew they still didn't have a winning record. The album just didn't capture Bette's multi-talented sound. At about the same time, Barry and Bette were doing a concert at Carnegie Hall. Barry managed to get a tape of the concert and he played it for Atlantic's Ahmet Ertegun. Ertegun realized immediately that this was the sound that was missing on the record. "Can you fix it?" he asked Barry.

Barry quickly forgot his bitterness and went back to the studio with as much enthusiasm as if it were for the first time. He ended up re-doing nine songs on the album. Manilow added the swaying, silly wonderful sound to "Chapel of Love," the exact amount of pathos to "Superstar," and the unusual character to the old ballad, "Delta Dawn." In Bette's words, "Barry made it special." In no time after its release, the record "went gold."

Even though Barry's arrangements made the difference on Bette's album, the sound was definitely hers. Barry doesn't impose what he wants to be on someone else. He knew how to let the real Bette Midler come forth. And in listening to Bette's first album, one can't help but wonder if he didn't purposely leave the raggedy edges on. Bette has said, "I don't want to ever be polished more than a little bit."

There was no doubt that Barry was a big help to Bette; yet he still knew what he himself was about. As the first album skyrocketed, and TV appearances on "The Tonight Show" increased the Midler craze, Barry Manilow made demonstration records of his own singing.

While Barry was selling his demos to Bell Records and signing a contract to do an album, Bette decided to go on tour again. At that point, Barry thought he was too busy to accompany her. But Bette was insistent and offered Barry the opportunity to perform three of his songs in the middle of her act. She also asked him to be her musical director. Performing in the middle of someone else's show is indeed a prime spot. After much consideration, Barry accepted.

The schedule proved to be too much. Barry found himself in the middle of his own album, completing a tour with Bette and beginning a second album with her. Bette's recording sessions ran from noon to six and Barry's sessions ran from seven till the early morning hours. He spent three straight months piggy-backing his recording sessions until he almost collapsed.

Yet pressure must be good for Barry's productivity. If Bette's first album was labeled a "compromise" between Barry Manilow and Joel Dorn, her second album could be labeled "all together." She feels, and so does Barry, that on the second album everything came together. On the first she was called "The Divine Miss M." On the second, she discarded a lot of the glitter and simplified her style to the sheer vocal ability of just Bette Midler.

Barry arranged and conducted all the songs on Bette's second album and co-produced it was with Arif

Mardin. The range of sounds is astounding— from the soft, heart-breaking version of "Surabaya Johnny" to the upbeat sounds of "Lullaby of Broadway" and "In the Mood." Barry had again arranged a gold winner for Bette Midler.

Simultaneously, Barry continued to find himself in the middle of Bette's act on her concert tour. So within one year's time, Barry had become a record-producer, composer, lyricist, recording and concert star, musical director, accompanist, and arranger. It was a full load to carry. And Barry's act was just beginning.

The 1973 concert tour with Bette Midler proved to be Barry Manilow's real debut. Their schedule involved not the usual little clubs; rather they were playing before audiences of eight or twelve thousand at state fairs. Barry and Bette programed the performance so that Bette would end the first act with Barry's arrangement of "Do You Wanna Dance?" The audience would be screaming and on their feet after Bette completed her number and then it was Barry's turn. Unannounced, unbilled, Barry Manilow proceeded to take his spot and do his three songs. It was a tough spot to be in— following Bette and performing without any billing. "So there was a lot of throwing up backstage, a lot of getting very, very sick," Barry moans.

There were some memorable times, though, on that tour. At an outdoor theater carved out of a mountain in Red Rock Amphitheatre in Colorado, Barry chose to sing one of the numbers from his first album, "Could It Be Magic." Somehow with the mountain setting, the open air and the real magic of his singing, Barry's audience was overwhelmed. The song differed completely from Bette's songs because of its classical arrangement

14

around a Chopin prelude. Despite the contrast with Bette's performance, the audience gave Barry his first standing ovation.

Bette's 1973 tour ended in December at the famous Palace theatre in New York. There was no doubt about it: if he hadn't been noticed before, Barry Manilow was certainly noted in the act at the Palace. Not everything always went smoothly, however, between Bette and Barry. And Bette frequently chose the stage upon which to vent her disagreements with Barry. Once in the middle of her act at the Palace, Bette looked at Barry and said, "Oh, Mr. Music, let's not do 'Surabaya Johnny' tonight, let's do 'Superstar' instead." Manilow did as he was asked, but Bette got the message that both he and the orchestra were upset with such a change in the middle of the show.

Offstage, Manilow and Midler minced no words or gestures with each other. They both say that ashtrays flew against walls, fists pounded on furniture, and Barry quite openly admits threatening to choke Bette if she pulled more stunts like that. But he knew that she would— and usually the very next night.

When the three-week engagement at the Palace was over, Bette said to her audience, "Good night, folks, I'm going out to lunch." With that, she stole off into obscurity to get some rest, privacy and perspective.

Bette Midler decided to retire for a while, and Barry Manilow decided to pick up on the Midler momentum. He then launched out on his own.

When Bette Midler is asked about Barry, the compliments run fast and frank. "Barry and I worked so fast. It was two ambitious people in one room," she laughs. "We would bitch at each other all the time," she

told reporters. "He very rarely did an arrangement I didn't like. He's a much better musician than I. We would mostly bicker about which song should go where and how the show should be paced. . . ."

Barry has no bitter feelings about the four and a half years he spent with Bette Midler. He's not that kind of person. His basic interest is in music and it looks as if he would do anything he could to help anyone, himself included, reach the potential desired in the music world.

When Barry left Bette's act, he walked into a career that was on the upbeat. And he walked in wearing success in silver shoes.

Jeans and a Blue Shirt

Though the accounts of Barry Manilow's life history are sketchy, it is clear that he has never thought of himself as a star. His first album opens with a scratchy, strange piece entitled "Sing It." Apparently, when Barry was three, his grandfather wanted him to be a star. He noticed that his grandson was musical and wanted to capitalize on that. He took young Barry to Times Square, to a little booth where one quarter in the slot gives you the time and the tape to make a record. Barry's grandfather wanted him to sing "Happy Birthday" for his cousin's birthday. But young Barry, who couldn't stop singing around the house, did not open his mouth. Hating to lose the quarter, the grandfather sang it himself. The recording on Barry's first album allows listeners this chance to hear the persuasion of a devoted grandfather and the protestations of a young grandson.

And somehow it also gives the listeners a feeling of simplicity about the performer who has since risen to fame.

Barry's father left him and his twenty-two year old mother when Barry was only two years old. "Grandma and Grandpa raised both of us," Barry is fond of saying. His grandparents also poured much music into his soul. At seven, he learned to play the accordion. He learned horas and old Russian folk music from them. And even he felt pretty proud of his version of "Lady of Spain" and "Tico Tico."

When he was 13, Barry's accordion was replaced by a piano. Barry likes to call it a birthday present— the piano came with his new stepfather. Willie Murphy, Barry's new father, did much to expand Barry's music exposure. One of the first things he did was take Barry to a Gerry Mulligan concert. "I'll never forget it," Barry said, "it was the biggest thing in my life." Hearing a baritone sax, after only hearing accordion music, opened a whole new world for Barry. With his new father also came a new stack of albums of vocalists and showtunes.

In time, Barry had real musical ambitions. "I wanted the piano to sound like a whole orchestra." And he wanted to be another Mancini, or at least an arranger for a very famous singer.

Though Barry lived in a poor area of New York while he was growing up, he never considered himself to be poor. In some ways, his family and music kept him rich. And often he had to fight to survive. "Even though it was a rough area and I got beaten up by the other kids," Barry reported, "I lived in a nice house and was treated with love by my parents and grandparents so I was never aware of being deprived."

Barry went to Brooklyn's Eastern District High School and was voted best musician of the school after his performance on the piano of De Falla's "Ritual Fire Dance."

After he finished high school, Barry still regarded his involvement in music as only a hobby. The thought of a professional career in music was far from his mind. He enrolled in a night advertising course at City College of New York and clipped ads at an ad agency during the day. Finding little satisfaction in that routine, he soon switched to New York College of Music and finally to the famous Juilliard School of Music. A job in the CBS mailroom paid the rent. Barry didn't mind going to school only at night because he still considered music his hobby.

But hobbies sometimes have a way of turning into careers. So at 18, Barry set himself up as a "musical handyman." He would write, arrange, produce and sing radio and TV jingles. He dabbled in writing themes for TV shows and working as musical director for a TV amateur show.

CBS offered Barry a job as film editor, but Barry turned it down in favor of his music. He wanted to be able to go on the road with cabaret singers. He enjoyed putting acts together and did one at this time with a female singer. "I was basically her arranger and accompanist, but on our first out-of-town act, they wanted a duo. So we said 'We're a duo!' " Soon after a two-year run at New York's Upstairs at the Downstairs, the "dynamic duo" split up.

In 1967, CBS called Barry back, and this time he accepted their offer. He became music director of the award-winning WCBS-TV talent series, "Callback!" He loved having the chance to do arrangements. He did 16

a week, arranging all kinds of numbers from rock to honky-tonk to opera. Barry learned timing, editing, everything involved in putting together a show. "Callback!" won an Emmy. Before long, Barry made a major breakthrough into big network and began conducting and arranging music for Ed Sullivan specials.

Also at CBS, Barry happened to meet a theatre director who asked him to do some musical arranging for one of his productions. In time, he was doing the coaching and directing of the music in an off-Broadway spoof musical called "The Drunkard." At first, Barry re-arranged old songs for these musicals, but he gradually replaced them with his original compositions. It was a great thrill for him to hear others sing his songs, for him to put harmonies together, to use horns and flutes, to add complexity to musical arrangements. Barry was hooked. Earlier he had been afraid to get into the musical business. Now he almost had no choice. It was quickly becoming his life.

Rarely did Barry turn down any opportunity involving music. In 1972, while Barry was substituting for the regular "house pianist" at the Continental Baths, an ad agency asked him to write a jingle for a TV commercial. Suddenly he was arranging commercials for products as diverse as toilet bowl cleaner to State Farm Insurance. "Clubs can't afford to pay me the $8000 it costs to keep the band going," Barry explained, "so the commercials subsidize the band."

Barry established a method for writing commercials. "It's a craft writing a jingle," he says, "because you have 28 seconds to get the message across and that's a whole lot different from writing a pop song. I usually write about ten jingles and the one I remember the easiest is the one I hand over to the company that wants it." Soon Barry found that he was making more money singing commercials than he was writing or arranging them, because Barry received a royalty each time one he sang appeared on TV. Most everyone has heard Barry sing the famous line from the McDonald commercial, "You deserve a break today. . . ."

The jingles were Barry's main source of income while he was arranging for Bette Midler. Then in 1973, Barry met Ron Dante at a commercial jingles session. They went out to lunch and Barry asked Ron to come back and listen to some of the rough cuts on Bette Midler's album.

"Actually it was Ron Dante's idea," Barry Manilow explained. "He insisted that I go and make some records of the songs I had written, because he liked them and he liked the way I sing. I really didn't care," Barry went on, "I was having a good time conducting and arranging for Bette, but we went ahead anyway."

At that point, everything could have turned in a different direction. Barry feels that he could have said, "Ronny, why don't you go in and sing 'Sweet Life' and we'll do the record for you." But Barry thought about it for a minute and imagined being back in the studio "with the strings and horns" and his fascination for music led him right into the search for $5000 to finance the record.

Besides "Sweet Life," Barry also recorded an upbeat, honky-tonk song, "Sweetwater Jones," and a purring, mellow song called "I Am Your Child." Bell Records bought the tapes, agreed to an album, and put a lot of money into promoting Barry. For his part,

22

Barry went on the road again. After several years of giving concerts with Bette Midler, Barry wasn't too happy to start on the treadmill again. Besides, this tour had much of the same flavor that Bette's did. Barry was using the same back-up musicians whom he had hired for Bette's tour.

However, there was no time for boredom. Soon after Barry's first album was released, Clive Davis took over Bell Records, changed the name to Arista, and found "Mandy" for Barry. Clive Davis is famous for making gold records almost immediately upon their release.

It must say something about Barry that at a time when Clive Davis was eliminating contracts, Barry was one of the few remaining musicians under contract. When Davis asked Barry to record "Mandy" as a single, Barry wasn't too interested. But Clive convinced him that if a ballad makes it big, the success surpasses that of a rock song. And Davis proved to be right. The single went to the top of the charts immediately and the second album from which it was taken followed.

"Mandy" was originally entitled "Brandy," but there was another song out by that name, so Davis changed the name to "Mandy" and decided on the ballad style. By early January, 1975, there was no doubt that "Mandy" was one of the recording industry's flawless commercial successes. Sometimes when a second album becomes successful, people go back and take another look at the first album. And that's exactly what happened to Barry's first album. At first it sold only 35,000 copies. But after "Mandy's" success, the hit from the first album, "Could It Be Magic," began rising sharply.

Although the song is unusually long, "Could It be Magic" seems to create a magical quality with its grandeur. Barry's lyrics and soft voice are a pleasant understatement to the magnificence of Chopin. Crescendo and decrescendo are used to give the piece its increasing and decreasing intensity. But never does Barry do too much. His mastery of pacing shows up constantly.

The variety in Barry's first album keeps the listener not quite sure of what kind of singer Barry is. Like Bette Midler, he is a master of rock, of ballad, honky-tonk and show tunes. He even recorded "Friends"— a song that was also on Bette Midler's first album. But unlike Bette, Barry not only arranges all his songs, he frequently writes the melodies and lyrics.

Many musicians applaud Manilow's use of chord progressions. These do not follow the same pattern in each song. In "Sweet Life," Barry sings the upbeat refrain of "Momma, can you hear me" in sharp contrast to the softer undercurrent of "I'm gonna live a sweet life." It seems, too, that Barry is not afraid to be romantic or to be labeled MOR— middle of the road. His albums show that he knows what he is about musically and he's not afraid to express that.

Barry Manilow doesn't create and arrange all the songs he sings. His second album shows just how well he works with songwriters, back-up musicians and even other arrangers. "Mandy" is a good example of how expressive Barry can be with someone else's song. Marty Panzer, an old high school friend, often writes the lyrics for Barry and since he knows Barry so well, the songs seem to fit Barry's style. "It's A Miracle," the other top-selling single from Barry's second album, is a combined effort of Marty and Barry's. Barry sings it with a real sense of spectacle — it's as if there really are people dancing in the street. When Barry appeared in Macy's Thanksgiving Day Parade in 1976, he and his trio sang "It's A Miracle." And while the TV camera was centered on Barry and the three women singers, viewers could still see bystanders dancing in the streets right along with the music.

It also sounds as if Barry has fun with some of the oldies he brings back, In "Avenue C," an old song made famous by Count Basie's big band, Barry sings all 32 back-up voices, which is a technical wonder in itself. In "The Two Of Us," which Barry and Marty Panzer composed together, Barry is able to make his voice express feelings of loneliness, resignation and frustration all at once. Most of the songs on this album do have a kind of show-tune quality. However, the definite rhythm-and-blues beat in "Early Morning Strangers" shows Barry can handle songs out of the MOR category.

Barry Manilow spends a lot of time giving credit where he feels it's due. He claims his lyricists as right arms. He calls his co-producer Ron Dante an unsung hero. "People never ask me enough about him, and I never give him enough credit, but he's my right hand. If I've got gold albums and singles, it's half him." Barry also feels that he couldn't have made it without Miles Lourie, his manager. "He has been with me before Bette. He's the one who had done it all with the career." The second album is dedicated to Lourie.

Obviously, Barry Manilow doesn't escape the critical pen of some reporters. An interviewer for "Rolling Stone" calls Manilow a "light crooner" who can make his voice crack at the most dramatic climax. It works best, the "Stone" interviewer says, in two ballads, "Early Morning Strangers" and "Mandy." "Both are enjoyable once one accepts their stagey self-pity."

Despite criticism, Barry talks and sings his philosophy. A song like "Something's Comin' Up," shows his attitude. He feels that there's always "something comin' up" in his life; he's not sure what it is or where it's leading him. But he has a strange feeling that "there's something dyin' and something being born" throughout the struggles of his life.

Whether Barry's on stage, recording an album or holding his favorite beagle, he seems to know and accept himself as a simple musician in jeans and a blue shirt.

White Tux

Barry Manilow know how to reach the masses with his music. He personally likes a rich variety of music but he knows what will sell. When Manilow bounds onstage— whether it's at Carnegie Hall or an outdoor fair in Pontiac, Michigan— he and his Lady Flash, captivate even the most reserved audiences. Throughout a show, Manilow moves with seemingly unlimited energy. One critic called Manilow a nightclubs owner's dream — "the act is energetic and enthused." And each show is linked together with personable conversation. Audiences end up not only wanting more of Barry's music but feeling as if they've known him for a long time.

Like Frank Sinatra, Barry Manilow is an interpretive singer. "You're Leaving Too Soon" and "Why Don't We Live Together," as well as the title tune from his third album, "Tryin' To Get The Feeling Again," show his uncanny ability to persuade listeners to accept his way of feeling. His presence on stage is loose and refreshing as he sometimes dances across the stage singing his own arrangements or as he sits at a high stool at the piano leading his own accompaniment. "Manilow doesn't bend to audience preconceptions," one reviewer said. "He puts his own taste, his own musicianship and his own personality on the line, and his audience snaps it up."

Even Barry's biggest hits, however can't compete with his commercials. His medley of commercials have become his trademark on the concert tour for over three years. Everyone recognizes the themes from Chevrolet, Dr. Pepper, Pepsi-Cola and McDonalds. Usually at the climax of the medley, a string of lights hanging from the piano around the footlights blink on and off in the Midler/Manilow camp style.

Despite the glitter, even the severest critics cannot deny that Manilow is constantly in charge; he's the headmaster of a sophisticated ensemble. His five-member back-up band, City Rhythm, are all hand-picked by Barry; and his choral trio, Lady Flash, add eye and sound appeal.

At the same time, no one, not even Barry's biggest fans, says that Manilow is going to lead the world into a new musical consciousness. People accept and generally like Barry's simple goals. He concerns himself with the importance of a show to go along with his music. His light-heartedness and his positive, genuine sense of professional delivery are the components of Manilow's show. Then, whether he is singing or talking between songs, Manilow impresses his audiences with his outright honesty. People like him because he's not a rip-off; there's nothing fake about him. He's a commercial artist who knows his trade unquestionably well.

Barry's fourth album, "This One's For You," produced early in 1976, became gold and nearly platinum immediately upon its release. Besides its sales, this album is noted for being an excellent pop album. It's a musical definition of where pop music is and where it's heading. He takes lyrics that might look banal and cliche out of context, and he makes them express sincere feeling. People who know Barry feel that many of his songs are autobiographical in feeling. Not all the songs are his own compositions, but they are usually those of his long-time friends or associates.

With Marty Panzer, Barry wrote "All The Time" in which he laments the time he wasted thinking that only he was all alone. In "Weekend In New England," Barry conveys the pain of separation — a feeling most people can identify with. There's no grand statement, no

suicide, no abandonment. In songs like that, Barry is credited for respecting the emotions of his audiences. He doesn't manipulate his listeners.

When Barry talks about his next album, he likes to think about doing something completely different. "I may move on, too, do a whole instrumental thing. This fourth album is all my own material. It's really a nice pop album," he told a reporter, "a step further than the last one. But you never know. I always live the struggle that comes with changing. . . "

It looks as if Barry's exposure will soon break away from just recordings and concert tours. He signed with ABC-TV to do his own special in February, 1977, along with Olivia Newton-John. Chances like that still amaze him. "I tell ya, I didn't expect that so soon. I'm brand new at this thing. I didn't think I was there yet."

Sometimes when he performs before record crowds he finds himself repeating to the audience, "I didn't expect you all. Are you sure you're not here for someone else?" Yet throughout 1976, Barry did amass acclaim and major awards, winning top male vocalist as well as being named "performer of the year" by "After Dark" magazine. And all of his records have either gone gold or platinum. That's quite a record for only two years in the spotlight.

When Barry is asked whether he likes being in the foreground, he replies, "Yeah, sure. Why not? I still consider it a job because of those many years of being in the background and having to be very solid— the brick, the guy that put it together." It seems that it's his stability that is a clue to his success, as Barry goes on to explain: "Because of all the discipline, I find it easier to do what I have to do, instead of being the freaked-out

30

artist." Barry is equally at ease with musicians, agents and audiences. "If I were a guitar player they found on the street and made into a star, I might not know how to handle it at all."

Yet a glance at his presence on stage shows that Barry is indeed accomplished and professional. With his flashy opening in sequins and silver shoes he proves that he does have a real show for his audience. Then, after a break, he returns in jeans and a blue shirt and performs without his band or Lady Flash. Quietly, at his piano, he plays the songs that he used to perform when he played piano in cocktail lounges.

Then, much in the same way Bette Midler did for him, Barry allows Lady Flash to solo. Later, he returns in his white tux and tails to sing some of his million-dollar songs, "Could It Be Magic," "Mandy," "It's A Miracle," and "I Write The Songs."

He does have a kind of magic, and it seems almost a miracle that he has risen to the top so fast. But mostly it's music that is the keynote to understanding Barry Manilow. Barry didn't write the lyrics to "I Write The Songs," but they are his message: "I've been alive forever . . . My home lies deep within you/And I've got my own place in your soul." That's what music means to Barry. And when he sings about the impact of music, its place in the development of people, its place in the human soul, it becomes clear that it is music that runs through Barry. It is music that keeps him alive. Even when he retreats from the spotlight or his name may be replaced by those of other stars, his craftsmanship with arrangements, his ability to help other musicians, and his inspirational attachment to music will keep Barry Manilow very much alive in the music world.

DIANA ROSS   JACKSON FIVE
THE OSMONDS   CARLY SIMON
CHARLIE RICH   BOB DYLAN
ELTON JOHN   JOHN DENVER
CHICAGO   THE BEATLES
FRANK SINATRA   ELVIS PRESLEY
BARBRA STREISAND   JOHNNY CASH
OLIVIA NEWTON-JOHN CHARLEY PRIDE
CAPTAIN AND TENNILLE ARETHA FRANKLIN
TONY ORLANDO   ROBERTA FLACK
BARRY MANILOW   STEVIE WONDER
DONNY AND MARIE   NEIL DIAMOND
SONNY AND CHER   CAROLE KING

Rock'n PopStars